Jamestown,

1607

Jamestown, 1607

MICHAEL L. COOPER

HOLIDAY HOUSE / *New York*

Library of Congress Cataloging-in-Publication Data
Cooper, Michael L., 1950—
Jamestown, 1607 / by Michael L. Cooper.—1st ed.
p. cm.
Includes bibliographical references.
ISBN-13: 978-0-8234-1948-7 [hardcover]
ISBN-10: 0-8234-1948-7 [hardcover]
1. Jamestown [Va.]—History—17th century—Juvenile literature.
2. Colonists—Virginia—Jamestown—History—
17th century—Juvenile literature. 3. Virginia—History—Colonial period,
ca. 1600—1775—Juvenile literature. I. Title.
F234.J3C66 2007
973.2′1—dc22
2006002018

To Ruth and Paul Frey, good people

Acknowledgments

I'd like to thank the third-grade class [2004—2005] at St. Patrick's Episcopal Day School in Washington, D.C., one of the best prepared audiences I've ever spoken to, for comments and suggestions on an early draft of Chapter 1. I'd also like to thank my aunt, Sharon Shelton, a retired English and writing teacher, for her careful editing of the manuscript.

Contents

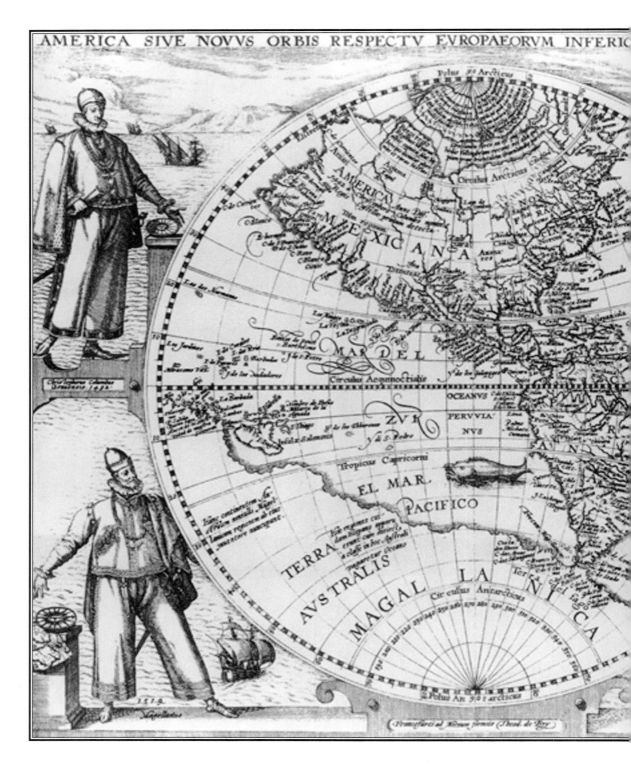

AMERICA SIVE NOVVS ORBIS RESPECTV EVROPAEORVM INFERIC

A 400-year-old map of the New World when Europeans knew little about South America or North America. The men in each corner are the prominent sixteenth-century explorers Christopher Columbus, Amerigo Vespucci, Ferdinand Magellan, and Francisco Pizarro.

Jamestown,

1607

Introduction:
Laying Claim to the New World

By the time England founded Jamestown in 1607, it lagged far behind its archrival Spain in claiming and profiting from its New World colonies.

Europeans dubbed the two continents, now known as North and South America, the New World. Christopher Columbus, while searching for a water route to Asia from 1492 to 1504, claimed all of the New World for Spain, except for a large chunk of South America that belonged to Portugal and would eventually become Brazil.

Spanish conquistadors such as Balboa, Cortez, and Pizarro conquered and enslaved tens of thousands of native people in Central and South America. They sent ships full of gold and silver back to Spain, quickly making it one of the world's richest and most powerful countries. In 1565 Spanish explorers founded St. Augustine in Florida, the first permanent European settlement in North America. Spain's presence did not stop France, Holland, and England from exploring North America and making their own claims.

The first sea captain to explore North America for the English was John Cabot, an Italian-born navigator. In 1497 he sailed along the coast of what is now Canada, looking for a water route, or northwest passage, between the Atlantic Ocean and the Pacific Ocean. On a second voyage the following year,

Cabot's fleet came as far south as the Chesapeake Bay. This bay, one of the largest in North America, lies between present-day Maryland and Virginia. On both trips Cabot claimed the land he saw for Britain.

WEAPEMEOC

A map of Roanoke Island drawn by John White,
a colonist who participated in two attempts to start
a colony there in the 1580s.

Nearly a century later, Sir Walter Raleigh, the famous explorer, named the land Virginia, in honor of England's Queen Elizabeth I. Her subjects called her the Virgin Queen because she never married.

England's first attempt to establish a colony came when Raleigh twice sent colonists to Roanoke Island in present-day North Carolina. The first group arrived in 1585, but unfriendly Native Americans and a lack of food forced them to leave after just a few months.

On the second attempt, over one hundred men, women, and children, led by John White, settled on the same wooded island in July of 1587. That fall White sailed back to England for supplies. He promised to return to Roanoke within six months, but a war with Spain delayed him for three years. White returned in 1590 and found the colony abandoned. There was no sign of the colonists. No one knows what happened to them. Some believe they went to live with the Croatian people who lived nearby. Others suspect the Croatians killed them. The failed Roanoke settlement became known as the Lost Colony.

The Englishmen who founded Jamestown in 1607 knew they faced hostile Native Americans and the challenge of surviving in the wilderness. But their dreams of discovering gold, founding a great city, and conquering new lands were stronger than their fears.

1. The First Day
in the Country Called Virginia

In April 1607, 105 colonists and 39 sailors crowded together in three small sailing ships that were being tossed about on the ocean by a cruel storm. These cold and wet men and boys had traveled nearly 7,450 miles since leaving England four months earlier. By now everyone had expected to be in the country they called Virginia. They must have feared they would never see land again.

John Ratcliffe, captain of the *Discovery,* urged Bartholomew Gosnold, captain of the *Godspeed,* and Christopher Newport, captain of the *Susan Constant,* to give up and return to England. But Newport, the fleet's commander, insisted on staying the course.

Finally, on the "six and twentieth day of April, about four o'clock in the morning, we descried the Land of Virginia," the colonist George Percy wrote. The sailor standing watch had heard the distant sound of waves slapping against sand, and word spread quickly. Soon sailors and colonists pressed against the railings, peering into the dark. They could smell the rich earth. As black night faded to gray dawn, Captain Newport guided the ships through the bay's twelve-mile-wide mouth. Earlier explorers had named it Chesapeake because that was the name of an Indian town at the mouth. Spanish, French, and English ships often skirted the coast, but few ever ventured into the bay.

These Englishmen had come to Chesapeake Bay to establish, or *plant* as they said then, a *plantation*, or colony, in Virginia. The country of Virginia stretched up the eastern seaboard from St. Augustine in Spanish Florida to

the French trading posts along the St. Lawrence River. The western boundary was not specific because no one then knew what lay inland.

The fleet sailed along the Chesapeake's western shore for about eight

Bartholomew Gosnold trading with the Native Americans in Virginia. This engraving by Theodor de Bry was first published in 1634.

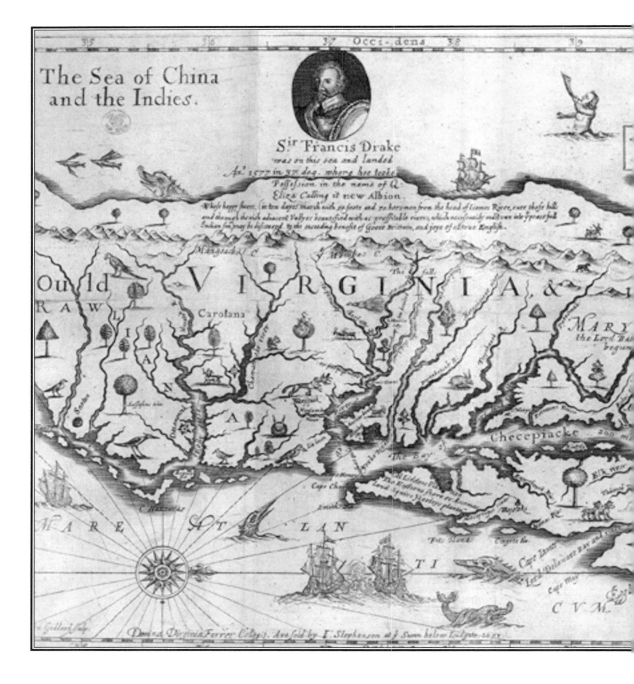

miles. At a spot today called Lynnhaven Bay, the three vessels rolled up their sails and dropped their anchors. After lowering two small boats into the blue-green water, some twenty men rowed ashore. The short, bearded Englishmen

A mid-seventeenth-century map of Virginia shows the Sea of China just beyond the mountains of western Virginia.

wore knee breeches and shiny chest armor. They carried swords and heavy single-shot muskets. Stepping out of their boats on that cool spring morning, the explorers warily scanned the sand dunes nearby and the woods beyond. English

people imagined the New World to be a land of grandeur and riches, as well as a place of horrible storms, deadly plants, ferocious animals, and man-eating natives.

As the sun climbed higher in the sky, the fear of attack faded away like the morning chill in the air. The men strolled along the beach, acting like kids on a field trip. They climbed sand dunes, plucked sea oats and bayberries while breathing the sweet smell of pine and cypress trees.

"Paradise," marveled Percy, describing the beautiful day and the land in his notes. "Fair meadows and goodly tall trees, with such fresh waters running through the woods."

At the end of the day, light from a nearly full moon sparkled on the water as the Englishmen walked to their boats. They must have dreaded leaving the sweet-smelling land and returning to their ships, crowded with men who had not bathed for weeks.

Suddenly "Savages creeping upon all Fours, from the Hills, like Beares, with their Bowes in their mouthes. Charged us very desperately," Percy later wrote. The men, dodging arrows from the bows of the five Native Americans, fired their muskets at the attackers. "After they had spent their Arrowes, and felt the sharpnesse of our shot, they retired into the Woods."

With two men wounded, the English rowed quickly to the safety of their ships.

Sir Walter Raleigh named Britain's colonial claim in North America "Virginia" to honor Queen Elizabeth I. Elizabeth's subjects called her the Virgin Queen because she never married. She ruled England from 1558 to 1603. This engraving, attributed to Hans Liefrinck, is from 1560.

2. A Glorious Possibility

THE JAMESTOWN EXPEDITION HAD SET OUT QUIETLY from London before dawn on Saturday, December 20, 1606. The expedition's three ships sailed down the Thames River to the English Channel.

The *Discovery*, the smallest ship, carried 21 sailors and colonists; the *Godspeed* carried 52; and the *Susan Constant*, the largest ship, carried 71. The ships rode low in the water because they were loaded with supplies that included tarps, building materials, a barge for river travel, cannons, swords, pikes [which are like spears], gunpowder, muskets, hatchets, gardening tools, and boxes of glass beads, small bells, and mirrors to trade with the Native Americans.

The Virginia Company of London, which was often referred to as the London Company, owned the fleet. This company was a new kind of business venture created to make money for shareholders. It was an early version of the modern corporation. Investors, who were called adventurers, bought shares in the company. In 1606 English King James I gave the company a royal charter, which was a legal statement of rights and responsibilities, to start a colony. Forty investors formed a council to run the venture. The London Company chose navigator Christopher Newport to command the fleet.

Newport was an old sea dog, someone who had been a sailor for a long time.

King James I became king of Scotland when he was only fourteen months old. He became England's king at age thirty-seven in 1603 and ruled until his death in 1625. This painting of James I is by Flemish artist Paul van Somer [1576—1621].

The Godspeed, Discovery, *and* Susan Constant *on the James River near Jamestown. This painting by Griffith Baily Coale dates from* 1949.

The forty-six-year-old man first crossed the Atlantic Ocean at age twenty. He served on an English privateer in the Caribbean, capturing ships carrying gold and silver from Spain's South American colonies. In one sea battle, an enemy

sailor had chopped off Newport's left hand. Despite the missing hand, he became a successful ship's captain.

Storms forced Commander Newport's fleet to spend a month on England's southern coast until the weather improved. Then the commander led his ships due south for 2,100 miles along the west coasts of France, Spain, and Portugal. Reaching northern Africa, the fleet turned west to the Canary Islands. They stopped there for supplies before beginning the 3,200-mile voyage across the Atlantic to the West Indies.

It was a typical ocean crossing of the time——ten weeks of being cold and wet, of enduring stench and sickness. The colonists and sailors lived together in ships with no more space than a typical classroom. They ate salted meat and fish. Their hardtack, a kind of biscuit, quickly became stale and infested by insects called weevils; the butter and cheese turned rancid. Even the drinking water, after a few weeks in storage, stank so badly a man had to hold his breath to swallow it.

Not surprisingly the colonists aboard the vessels were short-tempered. Arguments and fights were common. There was a terrible fight onboard the *Susan Constant* between John Smith and Edward Wingfield. The details are sketchy, but Smith later wrote that Wingfield accused him of trying "to usurp the government, murder the council, and make himself king." In other words Wingfield accused Smith of treason. It was a serious charge; people were shot or hanged for treason.

A "paire of gallowes was made, but Captaine Smith, for whome they were intended, could not be persuaded to use them," Smith wrote in his account of the voyage. Smith avoided execution, but beginning February 13 he was held prisoner for the rest of the voyage.

Wingfield, a gentleman descended from a family of knights, nobles, and other royal titles, was one of the expedition's most prominent members. Being a gentleman did not mean he was polite; it was a title. An upper-class Englishman often had a title such as esquire or gentleman. About half of the colonists who founded Jamestown were gentlemen. Wingfield looked down on Smith as the "son of a poor tenant." This attitude might have been the real reason for their fight because Smith did not tolerate disrespect.

John Smith was the son of a farmer. At age sixteen, after briefly serving as a merchant's apprentice, he joined the English army. For a decade Smith fought in wars in the Netherlands, France, and Hungary. He referred to his ten years of military experience as a university of war. This education would serve him well in Virginia. Smith's distinguished service earned him a coat of arms and the title of captain. Well-connected friends and a modest investment gave him a role in the Jamestown adventure. Smith devoted the rest of his life to what he called America's "glorious possibility."

In late March the three ships reached the West Indies. They stopped at several islands——Martinique, Dominica, Guadeloupe, Nevis, Tortola, and Mona——to collect fresh water and to hunt boars, iguana, and other wild animals for food. It was in these islands that one man, colonist Edward Brookes, died, probably of heat stroke. Transatlantic voyages were dangerous, and people often died because of disease, heat, or storms.

Newport left the West Indies and led his fleet into the Gulf Stream, an ocean current that flows up the east coast of North America. Nearly a month later, the ships entered Chesapeake Bay.

On April 30, four days after the surprise attack near Lynnhaven Bay, the English spotted five Native Americans on shore. Captain Newport called to them and placed his right hand over his heart. This gesture was a widely used sign for love or friendship. The Native Americans took the English to their village of Kecoughtan, near the spot known today as Old Point Com-

An engraving by Simon van de Pass [1595—ca.1647] shows John Smith wearing metal armor called a breastplate. The men at Jamestown wore breastplates to protect themselves from Native American arrows.

fort, where they were "entertained by them very kindly," Percy recalled.

Newport's fleet then continued along the western shore of the Chesapeake until coming to the mouth of a river that was nearly two miles wide. The Englishmen named it the James River in honor of King James.

On May 14, after exploring some forty miles of the newly named James River, Newport settled his colony a couple of miles below the mouth of another river, which the Native Americans called Chickahominy. He chose a strip of land about two miles long and a mile wide, covered by tall pine, oak, and willow trees. The men named the spit of land James Island and their encampment James Fort. Later it would simply become Jamestown. It was, Smith believed, "a very fit place for the erecting of a great city."

The Englishmen chose this spot because it appeared easy to defend from hostile Native Americans and from attacking Spanish ships. England and Spain were supposed to be at peace after decades of war. But now England was planting a colony on land claimed by Spain, so Newport wanted to be ready for a fight. The commander also liked the spot because the river was five fathoms, or thirty feet, deep. He wanted a site where trading ships could easily come and go.

Newport had already opened a box containing the list of men the investors had chosen to serve on a council to govern Jamestown. It's not clear why, but the names of these men had been kept secret until then. The councilors included two ships' captains, Gosnold and Ratcliffe. Little is known about Ratcliffe other than the fact that he had invested a lot of money in the London Company. Gosnold was one of the London Company's original founders and one of the expedition's most respected members. The council's other members were George Kendall, a soldier;

John Martin, a lawyer; and the two men who had quarreled during the voyage, Wingfield and Smith.

The colonists cut tree limbs and piled them in a semicircle to form a temporary fort. They were under orders from the London Company "not to offend the Naturals," or Native Americans, so they did not build a proper fort. The colonists also built a cabin where Chaplain Robert Hunt conducted Church of England services every morning and evening. For themselves the men made simple shelters of tree branches or dug holes and covered them with canvas. They later built small houses of wood and mud.

The London Company had included craftsmen and laborers among the colonists because they had skills needed to help build and protect the colony. There were four carpenters, two bricklayers, one blacksmith, one mason, one tailor, one surgeon, and a sail maker. The company wanted to earn a profit for its investors by starting industries such as glassmaking and by cutting trees for lumber. After seven years of working for the London Company, these craftsmen and laborers would be given land so they would be able to work for themselves.

The council elected Wingfield president for a one-year term. As president, Wingfield would be responsible for the day-to-day running of the colony. Next the councilmen voted to deny Smith a seat because of his earlier quarrel with Wingfield. Smith was no doubt angry, but he had to accept the council's decision. Meanwhile there was much work to be done.

3. Looking for Gold

THE COUNCIL MEMBERS had specific written instructions from the London Company: The colonists were to plant gardens to feed themselves and to look for survivors of the Lost Colony. They also were to establish trade with the native people, whom they considered savages, while encouraging them to abandon their traditional ways and become Christians.

The company also wanted answers to two questions: Was there gold in Virginia? Was there a northwest passage to the Pacific Ocean? The London Company ordered Newport to take forty men, spend two months exploring, and then return to England by summer's end with answers to these questions.

Newport could not follow these orders faithfully because there was not enough time to explore for eight weeks if he was to make the long transatlantic voyage before fall. More importantly, the commander was afraid to take so many men away from Jamestown, leaving it vulnerable to attack. He had good reason to worry.

Soon after the English tied their ships to the trees on James Island, some three dozen Algonquin warriors from the Paspahegh village a few miles upriver brought them "a Fat Deare as a gift." The colonists accepted the venison warily. Why, they wondered, were so many armed men delivering one dead deer? The settlers really became suspicious when the men wanted to spend the night. Newport said no, and the warriors left angry. "They came," Percy noted, "more in villainy than any love they bare us."

The Paspaheghs were mad because the colonists were building Jamestown on land where the tribe once had a village. The Englishmen, as ignorant of Native American customs as the Native Americans were of English customs, only saw uninhabited land. Native Americans did not own land by deeds and written laws. But most tribes, reasonably enough, wanted a few miles of space around their villages where they could hunt, farm, and feel safe. They defended their territory from other tribes.

Despite the threat of attack, Newport decided to spend a week looking for gold and for a northwest passage. He took only twenty-three men with him. Among them was John Smith, who had finally been given his seat on the council. He was too valuable to keep confined. Smith learned some of the Algonquin language from Englishmen who had learned it from Croatians on Roanoke Island. He kept a list of Algonquin words that he added to and studied. This word list is one of only two surviving lists of the Algonquin dialect spoken by local tribes.

Newport's party set out in the colony's barge on May 21, 1607. "Thus from James Fort we took our leave about noon," wrote Gabriel Archer, the official note taker for the trip, "and by night we were up the river eighteen mile. . . ." The men rowed past the hostile Paspahegh town and spent their first night in a Weanoc village where they were welcomed with a feast. Newport gave his hosts bells and red glass beads, which the Weanocs prized.

News of the Englishmen and their gifts spread upriver. The following day as the explorers rowed by, clusters of cheering men and women, boys and girls gathered on the riverbanks. They held up baskets of bread, dried oysters, and roasted venison, hoping the English would stop to trade.

Newport's party passed numerous towns. "They live commonly by the waterside," Archer wrote in his notes, "in little cottages made of canes and reeds, covered with the bark of trees."

The English stopped at several towns and each time the greeting was similar. Crowds of thirty to forty villagers gathered and shouted words of welcome. The village werowance, which is the Algonquin word for "chief," gave "an oration testifying their love" as women prepared platters of bread, turkey, and venison. After the feast the Englishmen and Native Americans shared clay and copper pipes full of strong tobacco. Then, Percy wrote, the villagers "entertained us with dances and much rejoicing." The dancers shouted, howled, and stamped "against the ground like so many wolves or devils."

The Algonquin looked very different from the English. The men were at least six feet tall, a half-foot taller than the average Englishman. Both men and women were muscular with straight, stately posture, black hair, and dark eyes. When it was warm, adults and children went about naked, or covered their "privities with beasts skins." In cold weather everyone wrapped themselves in skins and fur.

The warriors scraped all of the hair off the right sides of their heads so it would not become tangled in their bows. But they let the hair on the left sides grow to shoulder length; the Englishmen called this style a scalp lock because it made scalping a dead enemy easier.

Men and women wore feathers, copper, bones, and shell beads like jewelry. Some sported birds' legs dangling from holes in their ears. They decorated

their bodies with tattoos, body piercing, and paint made from plants. The bright colors were, Archer observed, "very beautiful and pleasing to the eye." The children's skin was whiter than the tawny or reddish skin of adults. The red skin, the English learned, was the result of years of rubbing their bodies with bear grease, walnut oil, and berry juice.

About seventy-five miles up the James, the explorers "came to an overfall impassable for boats any further. Here the water falls down through great main rocks," Archer wrote. The Arrohattoc tribe lived there in a hilltop village called Powhatan, which was surrounded by fields of tobacco, corn, beans, and gourds.

On the trip Newport had heard about a werowance named Powhatan who ruled some thirty tribes occupying more than fifty towns along the James, Chickahominy, and Pamunkey rivers. The English referred to Powhatan as king or emperor; he was clearly the most powerful leader in the region.

Because of the town's name, Newport thought it was Powhatan's home. Instead the commander met a werowance named Pawatah who warned the explorers against going farther upriver into the mountains because a fierce tribe called Manoc lived there.

Assuring Pawatah that he could "terrify and kill" his enemies, Newport demonstrated his weapons. When a soldier fired his musket, Archer wrote, Pawatah "stop'd his ears, and express'd much fear, so likewise all about him. Some of his people being in our boat leapt overboard at the wonder hereof."

Native American men and women fishing from a dug-out canoe. The men in the background are spearfishing. The fence on the left is called a weir, which was used to trap fish. This drawing is by John White circa 1580.

They seemed to fear the noise more than the bullets. Newport promised that he would "never use this thunder" against his friends.

The Native Americans also told Newport about a large body of water just beyond the mountains. It's not clear what they were talking about, but Newport believed it was the long-sought northwest passage.

The Englishmen were excited about another discovery. While exploring around the falls, Smith found "veins of glistering spangles" among the rocks. The Jamestown colonists desperately wanted to enrich themselves and their nation. Newport believed the mountains were full of gold, and he wanted to rush samples of the ore back to London.

Going back downstream to Jamestown, the explorers met two important chiefs. One of them was a woman; women chiefs were rare.

"We saw the queen of this country," Archer noted. "She is a fat, lusty, manly woman. She had much copper about her neck, a crownet [crown] of copper upon her head; she had long black hair, which hanged loose down her back to her middle, which only part was covered with a deer's skin, and else all naked." Archer did not record her name; perhaps he couldn't spell it. Historians believe the woman was Opossunoquonuske, werowance of the Appomattocs and one of Powhatan's sisters. When the Englishmen were leaving, Opossunoquonuske suggested they stop downriver to meet one of her brothers, a werowance named Opechancanough.

Opechancanough welcomed the Englishmen warmly. After a feast and dancing, boys entertained the visitors by diving into the river for mussels and prying open the sharp shells to find pearls. Then an incident occurred that reminded the English not to forget this was hostile country. The werowance asked Newport to walk alone with him into the woods. The English suspected

The *Algonquin village Secota* on the *Pamlico River* some sixty miles south of *Jamestown. The scene depicts a prosperous village of wigwams and gardens as well as a lively social life, as the group of dancers suggests. Theodor de Bry copied this engraving from a John White drawing and published it in* 1594.

a trap, so they followed the pair. When Opechancanough saw he was being followed, he abruptly ended the walk and whatever trap he might have had planned.

The next morning as the explorers neared Jamestown, the Native Americans they met near Point Weanoc seemed sullen and nervous. This behavior made the Englishmen fear "some mischief at the Fort." They hurried downriver. The group arrived on Wednesday, May 27, and learned that a day earlier hundreds of warriors had attacked the colony. The attackers killed one boy and wounded eleven men, one of whom later died. Only cannon fire from the *Susan Constant* saved the colony.

Newport now ignored the London Company's order about offending "the Naturals" and told his men to build a triangular fort, or palisade, of tall upright logs. They placed four or five small cannon in each corner of the palisade. Hostile Native Americans lurked in the woods, making it dangerous to leave the fort. Eastace Clovill made the mistake of going into the woods, perhaps "to doe naturall necessity," or use the bathroom. He stumbled back to the fort with six arrows piercing his body and died a week later.

In late June, Newport took the *Susan Constant* and the *Godspeed,* and sailed for England. In London the commander told the investors that the "country is excellent and very rich in gold and copper."

But back in Jamestown, life was anything but excellent.

4. Such Misery

DISEASE AND STARVATION KILLED over half the colony that first summer. "There were never Englishmen left in a foreign country in such misery as we were in this new-discovered Virginia," lamented George Percy.

Percy kept a list of the men who died during three weeks in August:

"The sixth of August, there died John Asbie of the bloody flux.

"The ninth day, died George Flower of the swelling.

"The tenth day, died William Bruster, gentleman, of a wound given by the savages, and was buried the eleventh day.

"The fourteenth day, Jerome Alikock, ancient [a military rank equal to ensign], died of a wound; the same day, France Midwinter; Edward Moris, corporal, died suddenly."

In just twenty-two days, nineteen men had died.

Native Americans killed some of the men on Percy's list. But most died because hunger and polluted drinking water made them weak and vulnerable to disease. Every day the colonists ate the same meager meal. "Our food was but a small can of barley sod in water to five men a day," Percy wrote. Squirming white worms infested the barley. These tiny worms were beetle or moth larvae that often hatch in stored grain. The starving settlers ate the barley, worms and all.

"Our drink cold water taken out of the river, which was at a flood very salt, at a low tide full of slime and filth," Smith explained. It was "the destruction of many of our men." The river water caused painful swelling and deadly typhoid and dysentery, or "bloody flux."

The survivors buried the dead at night to hide the deaths from Powhatan's people who always seemed to be watching from the woods. The colonists were afraid the natives would see how weak they had become and attack. However, in late summer it was the Native Americans who rescued the colony. "It pleased God," Smith acknowledged, "after awhile to send those people which were our mortal enemies to relieve us with victuals, as bread, corn, fish, and flesh in great plenty." That help, Smith believed, saved the colony.

As children the Algonquins had learned to be skilled hunters, fishermen, and farmers, and they worked constantly to feed their villages; but the colonists were less industrious. "They would rather starve and rot with idleness" than work, Smith complained frequently. Few of the Englishmen, especially the gentlemen, wanted to plant gardens, build houses, or hunt. There was plenty of game in the woods, but the colonists were not good at tracking and slaying a deer or any wild animal.

Smith sarcastically criticized the Jamestown residents for laziness. "Though there be fish in the sea, foules in the ayere, and beasts in the woods . . . and we [are] so weake and ignorant, we cannot much trouble them. . . ."

As if the lack of food was not enough of a problem, bitter arguments split the colony into factions. Bad leadership, Smith charged, pointing a finger at President Wingfield, caused many of the problems. The settlers, Smith said in his notes, accused the president of hoarding food and "of feasting himself."

On September 10, the three surviving council members——Smith, Ratcliffe, and Martin——confronted Captain Wingfield and removed him from the presidency. The council appointed Ratcliffe president and Smith cape merchant, which meant he was in charge of supplies and food.

The new president immediately ran into his own problems. Ratcliffe argued with James Read, a blacksmith. It's not clear why the two men argued. But Read threatened to hit the president. It was just a threat, but a serious crime nonetheless. The same laws that governed people in England governed people in Jamestown. Read's threat was a crime because the president represented the king.

After a quick trial, a jury found the blacksmith guilty and decided he should be hanged. As the executioner led Read to the gallows, the condemned man blurted out an astonishing confession: Captain Kendall was a Spanish spy. Read was spared.

The president put Kendall on trial. The jury heard the evidence and found him guilty of planning to steal the ship and sail it to Spanish Florida. A firing squad promptly executed him.

Meanwhile the new cape merchant needed to solve Jamestown's gravest problem, the lack of food. But when Captain Smith visited the neighboring werowances, they refused to trade food for beads and bells. They wanted only hatchets and swords. Smith did not want to give the tribes weapons. He decided it was time to meet Powhatan.

5. Facing the Great Chief

IN EARLY DECEMBER OF 1607, Captain Smith and nine men set out to find Powhatan. They traveled some fifty miles up the Chickahominy River. When the river became too shallow for their barge, Smith hailed two Native Americans passing in a dugout canoe. The pair agreed to take Smith, John Robinson, and Thomas Emry upriver.

The remaining men waited with the barge. One of them, George Cassen, went ashore and into the woods where warriors grabbed him and demanded to know where the white chief, meaning Smith, had gone. Cassen refused to tell, so the natives tied him to a tree. Using sharp reeds and sharp mussel shells, they cut off the Englishman's fingers and toes. Cassen screamed out that Smith had gone upriver to find Powhatan. But his captors didn't stop. They scalped Cassen, peeled the flesh from his face, and ripped open his stomach, while others piled wood around his feet, preparing to burn him alive.

Meanwhile, some of the warriors raced upriver to catch Smith. They found Robinson and Emry cooking food over a fire. Smith and one of his native guides were exploring nearby when they heard screams coming from the direc-

Native Americans surround Smith and his guide. This illustration appeared in John Smith's book, The General History of Virginia, *published in 1624.*

Their C.S triumph about him

C: Smith bound to a tree to be shott to death
1607.

How they tooke him prisoner in the Oaze 1607

C. S.

C. S.

C. Smith bindeth a saluage to his arme, fighteth with the King of Pamaunkee and all his company, and slew 3 of them.

Another illustration from John Smith's book shows him being taken captive by Opechancanough.

tion of the fire. The captain pulled out his pistol and grabbed his guide to use as a shield as they faced a swarm of warriors with their bows drawn. While dodging arrows Smith shot and killed three of his attackers. The captain and his guide slowly backed up until he stumbled into a creek. The freezing water soon made Smith numb, and he tossed his gun on the ground, surrendering.

Captain Smith expected to be tortured or killed outright. He was surprised to discover that Opechancanough, the werowance Smith had met a few months earlier, led the attackers. The chief treated Smith well, but the captain saw that John Robinson, with twenty to thirty arrows in him, had been killed. Smith did not report the fate of his guides, but it was learned later that Emry had been killed.

The warriors took Smith to their Pamunkey River village where, he later reported, "Each morning three women presented me with three great platters of fine bread, [and] more venison than ten men could devour." The prisoner and his guards even became friendly.

There was one scary incident. The father of a warrior killed by Smith tried, as was the custom, to avenge his son's death. But guards stopped him.

After three weeks Opechancanough took Smith to Werowocomoco where Powhatan lived. Werowocomoco consisted of some one hundred wigwams clustered on a hill. *Wigwam* is an Algonquin word that means "lodge or dwelling." The wigwams were oval- or box-shaped homes made of poles covered with thatched-reed mats. An ordinary dwelling was about the size of a small house trailer.

The great chief, of course, did not live in an ordinary wigwam. A wall of vertical logs, similar to the palisade enclosing Jamestown, surrounded Powhatan's home. The werowance's wigwam stretched for nearly 150 feet, or about half of the length of a football field. Powhatan lived there with his many wives and children.

Smith, the first European ever to see this Native American king, described Powhatan:

"[T]heir emperour proudly lying upon a bedstead a foot high, upon ten or twelve mats, richly hung with many chains of great pearls about his neck, and covered with a great covering of Rahaughcums [raccoon skins]. At his head sat one woman, at his feet another. On each side, sitting upon a mat upon the ground, were ranged his chief men on each side of the fire, ten in a rank, and behind them as many young women."

Smith was impressed by Powhatan's majesty.

While priests, wives, and children watched, the werowance questioned

Smith. He especially wanted to know why the Englishmen had come to his land. Smith did not want to reveal that he hoped Jamestown would be the first of many English colonies in Virginia. So he explained that a storm had driven them into the Chesapeake, and they would leave when Commander Newport returned.

This village near Roanoke, drawn by John White circa 1850, probably resembles Powhatan's village and palisade.

The captain then tried to impress Powhatan by describing Newport as the werowance of all the waters and a fierce warrior.

While Smith bragged about Newport's strength, Powhatan's priests began chanting loudly. Men carrying heavy stones followed by fierce-looking warriors armed with clubs filed into the middle of the lodge. They grabbed Smith, forced him to kneel, and pressed his head against the stones. The captain must have been expecting the clubs to crush his skull when he heard a girl's cry. Powhatan spoke sternly to the girl; but she ignored him, darted from the crowd, and knelt by Smith. The child took "his head in her arms and laid her own upon his to save him from death."[1]

This girl was Pocahontas, Powhatan's favorite daughter. Pocahontas wanted her father to spare the prisoner's life. After arguing briefly with his daughter, Powhatan agreed.

The werowance kept Smith confined for two days before bringing him back to the big wigwam. There, sitting in the dimly lit room, the captain heard the "most dolefullest noise." Then dozens of warriors entered the lodge disguised in a "fearful manner." Powhatan, like the men with him, was painted black and looked more "like a devil than a man."

After chanting and dancing, Powhatan explained that Smith was now his adopted son and a werowance with the Algonquin name of Nantaquaus. He added that he expected his son, like his other werowances, to send him gifts as a tribute. Specifically, Powhatan wanted two cannon and a grindstone to sharpen his growing store of axes and swords.

He "sent me home with four men," Smith explained, "one that usually carried my gown and knapsack after me, two others loaded with bread, and one to

King Powhatan comands C. Smith to be slayne, his daughter Pokahontas beggs his life, his thankfullnes and how he subiected 39 of their kings. reade ý history.

A drawing from John Smith's The General History of Virginia *shows Pocahontas coming to his aid, circa 1623.*

accompany me." They walked the twelve miles through the forest to the colony.

At Jamestown, Smith was welcomed by almost all of the colonists. He was not welcomed by Archer and Ratcliffe who charged the captain with the deaths of Robinson and Emry.

"Great blame . . . was laid upon me by them for the loss of our two men which the Indians slew." Smith later suspected the president and his allies were unhappy because they had planned to steal the ship, desert the colony, and sail to England. They knew Smith would stop them.

Ratcliffe gave the captain a quick trial; the jury found him guilty and ordered that he be shot by a firing squad. "But in the midst of my miseries," Smith was no doubt happy to write, "it pleased God to send Captain Nuport [Newport]."

6. Cursed Gold

ON HIS RETURN TO JAMESTOWN on January 2, 1608, Commander Newport stopped Smith's execution. While Newport was in Virginia, the commander took charge of the colony. He was not interested in executing anyone.

First, Newport wanted to get new colonists settled. The *Susan Constant* had brought between eighty to one hundred men to Jamestown [the exact number is uncertain]. This group, known as the first supply, included thirty-three gentlemen, twenty-one laborers, four tailors, one surgeon, two apothecaries, a gunsmith, a goldsmith, a blacksmith, two refiners, a perfumer, a jeweler, and a cooper, which is a barrel-maker. The first supply also included forty people on a second ship, the *Phoenix*. But that ship had been lost in a fog a week earlier. It was not unusual for a ship to be delayed by bad weather, and Newport expected it to show up soon.

The commander was intent on finding gold. The ore gathered the previous summer had proven to be an embarrassment. After Newport had confidently informed the London Company that Virginia was rich in gold, an assayer [a specialist in analyzing minerals and precious ores] reported that the glittering rocks did not contain a speck of gold. The glitter was iron pyrite, which is also called fool's gold. Angry investors accused Newport of chicanery, or trickery.

The commander now feared that if Jamestown proved unprofitable, the London Company would remove the settlers and abandon the colony. New-

This Theodor de Bry engraving copied from a John White sketch depicts an Algonquin chief.

port wanted to resume his search for gold, as soon as the new men were settled.

These newcomers and the thirty or so surviving original settlers were building shelters when, on January 7, fire destroyed most of Jamestown. No one knows how the fire started. But it reduced the wood-and-thatched-roof buildings and everything in them——books, clothing, and food——to smoldering ashes. That fire left some 150 men in midwinter with little food and no shelter. "Many of our old men diseased and [many] of our new for want of lodging perished," Smith reported.

The Native Americans were again, literally, lifesavers. "The Emperor

Powhatan each week once or twice sent me many presents of deer, bread, rau-groughcans [raccoons]," Smith recalled. "[V]ictuals, you must know, is all of their wealth, and the greatest kindness they could show us." The captain believed the Native Americans saved Jamestown that dreadful winter.

Pocahontas often brought the food. Smith described her as a unique "child of ten years old which not only for features, countenance, and proportion much exceedeth any of the rest of his [Powhatan's] people." The tough soldier, who never married or had children, teased and played games with her. He adored the girl as though she were a favorite niece.

By late February the colonists had hastily constructed crude shelters from tree branches, canvas, and other scraps of material. Newport then took Smith and some thirty other men, along with boxes of beads, pins, bells, and cloth, and set off to see Powhatan. Newport believed he could use Smith's friendship with Pocahontas and her father to help him find gold. If anyone knew where to find the ore, the commander reasoned, it would be Powhatan.

At Werowocomoco, Captain Smith led twenty men into the village to make sure it was safe. They were armed with muskets and swords, and wore quilted leather jackets, called jacks, to protect them from arrows. But the townspeople were friendly. Clusters of men and women cheered as the Englishmen walked among the wigwams to Powhatan's compound. "Before his house stood forty or fifty great platters of fine bread." This was a good sign. A platter of bread was a traditional Algonquin symbol of welcome.

Inside Powhatan's wigwam, Smith saw the werowance adorned with pearls, copper, and feathers, and reclining on a couch of animal skins. "This proud savage," Smith wrote, had "a majesty as I cannot express nor yet have often seen either in pagan or Christian."

A Theodor de Bry engraving of Native Americans in Florida looking for gold reflects the widespread belief among Europeans that gold was plentiful in the New World. The Jamestown colonists were obsessed with finding gold.

Powhatan immediately beckoned for Smith to sit next to him. Together they listened as several warriors made speeches declaring the tribe's friendship with the English. Powhatan told Smith that they all should share "the corn, women, and country." Everyone then feasted on turkey, bread, and water. Afterward Smith gave the chief several gifts, including items fashionable in England such as a red wool suit, a white greyhound dog, and a hat.

The following day, for his first meeting with Commander Newport, Powhatan prepared an even grander feast. The commander gave the werowance another gift, thirteen-year-old Thomas Savage. Not wanting to be outdone, Powhatan gave Newport a young man named Namontack. Both Savage and Namontack were to live among each other's countrymen in order to learn their languages and customs. According to Smith, Namontack had "a shrew's subtle capacity" that he used "to know our strength and our country's condition." Despite all of the gifts and declarations of friendship, the captain did not trust Powhatan. Smith suspected that the chief was just waiting for the right opportunity to destroy Jamestown.

Smith watched uneasily while the commander and the werowance traded. The old chief was a much better trader. Smith became concerned that Newport swapped too many copper cooking pots and hatchets for too few baskets of corn. The captain intervened by letting Powhatan glance at a string of dark-blue glass beads. Powhatan immediately wanted the beads. But Smith said no, they were too rare. This made the werowance want them even more. Smith finally agreed to trade a pound of beads for two hundred bushels of corn.

After they had finished trading, Powhatan told Newport where to look for gold, a spot about twenty miles upriver. The English spent several days digging among the rocks. Smith complained that there "was no talke, no hope, no worke, but dig gold, wash gold, refine gold, loade gold." The captain had little patience for this gold fever. He wanted the colonists to spend more time growing food, building houses, and making the Jamestown colony secure.

Newport's prospecting party returned to Jamestown the second week of March, loaded the rocks onto his ship, and prepared to sail back to England. As a going-away gift, Powhatan sent Newport twenty turkeys. In return, Newport generously sent Powhatan twenty swords. In early April the *John and Francis,* carrying Namontack, Gabriel Archer, Edward Maria Wingfield, and several other colonists who were weary of the difficult life in Jamestown, disappeared down the King's river.

Ten days later Captain Frances Nelson and the *Phoenix* finally appeared. Nelson explained that, after losing Newport's ship in the fog, he had sailed to the Caribbean to spend the winter. Nelson only stayed about thirty days in Virginia. Smith sent a shipment of logs back to London on the *Phoenix.* The logs would be worth more, Smith felt, than all of the rocks on Newport's ship.

Smith also gave Nelson a report called "A True Relation." It described the colony's first year and included a rough map of the Chesapeake Bay region. When the report reached England, it sparked widespread interest in the Jamestown colony and encouraged more people to seek passage to Virginia.

During the summer of 1608, Smith and twenty other men explored the big bay. They hoped to find the northwest passage and discover great cities like the Aztec metropolises the Spanish had found in Mexico.

The explorers found neither a shortcut to the Pacific nor grand cities, but they did see a land of incredible natural beauty and bounty. The woods were "extreme thick full of wolves, bears, deer, and other wild beasts," Smith wrote.

They explored a river that would be named the Potomac, after a local Native American tribe. It was full of fish "lying so thick with their heads above the water, as for want of nets [our boat driving amongst them] we attempted to catch them with a frying pan." It was, Smith observed dryly, "a bad instrument

to catch fish with." The men had more success spearing fish with their swords, until an accident nearly killed the captain.

While Smith was removing a stingray from his sword, it whipped its long tail around and stung him with its poisonous barbs. The "torment was so

A map of the Chesapeake region drawn by John Smith.

instantly extreme," the captain recalled, that he soon fell ill and his hand, arm, and shoulder swelled to nearly twice normal size. Smith thought he was going to die. He even chose his burial spot on a bit of land he later dubbed Stingray Point. But by evening the swelling had gone down, and Smith felt well enough to eat the stingray for dinner.

Smith was the first European to explore, survey, and map the big bay. Several parts of the Chesapeake, such as Stingray Point and Smith Island in the lower bay, still bear the names Smith gave them.

When the explorers returned to Jamestown on July 21, they must have immediately longed for the peacefulness out on the bay. The new colonists were sick for lack of what they called "seasoning." Their bodies had yet to adapt, or become seasoned, to the weather, water, and diseases of the New World. And everyone was angry with President Ratcliffe for wasting precious food and for making them build him a house so elaborate that they called it a palace.

The settlers wanted to kick Ratcliffe out of office. The three surviving councilmen——Martin, Smith, and Scrivener——decided that Scrivener would serve as temporary president until September and then Smith would become president. Captain Smith returned to exploring the bay for eight more weeks before he assumed his new responsibilities.

7. Powhatan's Strange Coronation

SHORTLY AFTER JOHN SMITH BECAME Jamestown's new president on September 10, 1608, Commander Newport arrived aboard the *Mary and Margaret* with Namontack and seventy new colonists, the second supply.

The newcomers included Mistress Forrest and Anne Burras, the first Englishwomen at Jamestown. Several weeks later, in the first wedding in Virginia, Burras married John Laydon, one of the few original colonists still alive.

In addition to the usual missions of finding Roanoke survivors, a northwest passage, and gold [the last load of rocks had contained no more gold than the first], Newport had an additional, and somewhat curious, assignment. He had instructions to crown Powhatan king. Apparently the London Company thought a formal coronation would flatter the werowance and make him more cooperative.

Smith and four other men walked through the forest to Werowocomoco. They invited Powhatan to Jamestown for the coronation. Powhatan was suspicious, and he refused to leave his village.

A few days later Newport, Smith, and some fifty men took the barge to Werowocomoco to hold the coronation ceremony. First, Newport presented gifts to the werowance, including a washbasin and pitcher, a bed, and clothing

The English coronation of Powhatan was an attempt to win favor with the powerful Algonquin chief.

that the English considered civilized. Despite the presents, Powhatan only grudgingly participated in the ceremony. He refused to kneel to be crowned. Finally one man pressed heavily on the werowance's shoulder, forcing him to bend his knees ever so slightly, and Newport quickly placed the crown on Powhatan's head.

To celebrate the coronation, the men on the barge fired a cannon. The loud *ka-boom* caused panic among the townspeople and worsened Powhatan's mood. He gave the English only fourteen baskets of corn and said no to the commander's request for warriors to guide him to the mountains beyond the James River falls.

Smith complained that the coronation had been a bad idea. "For we had his favor much better only for a plain piece of copper till this stately kind of soliciting made him so much overvalue himself that he respect[ed] us as much as nothing at all."

Several weeks after the coronation, Newport and 120 armed men took a trip into the mountains some forty miles beyond the falls to look for gold and for the big body of water the Native Americans said lay just beyond the mountains. Newport hoped it was the Pacific Ocean. They found neither gold nor ocean, and after a week returned to the falls.

Newport had expected to get supplies from the people in the village of Powhatan, but they refused and hid their corn and other food. Newport arrived back at Jamestown with 120 hungry men. Smith worried about the colony's dwindling food supply and about the Algonquins' growing hostility.

Native Americans frequently visited Jamestown and secretly swapped valuable furs with colonists and sailors for weapons and tools. The warriors also

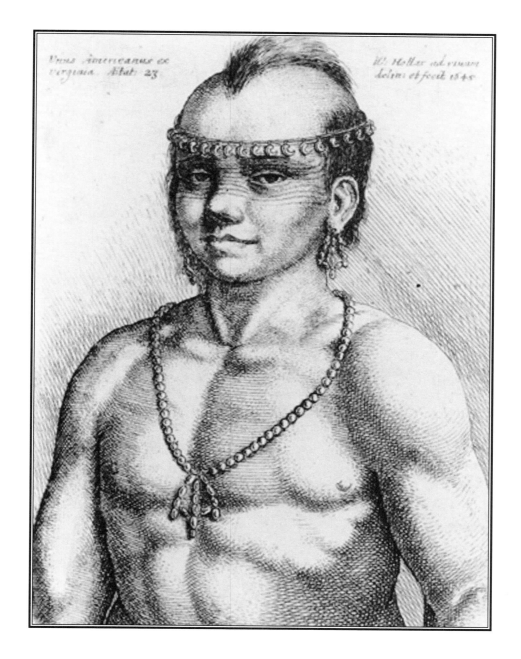

An engraving by Theodor de Bry of a young Algonquin warrior

A
TRVE RE-
lation of such occur-

rences and accidents of noate as
hath hapned in Virginia since the first
planting of that Collony, which is now
resident in the South part thereof, till
the last returne from
thence.

Written by Captaine Smith *Coronell of the said Collony, to a
worshipfull* friend of his in England.

LONDON

Printed for *Iohn Tappe*, and are to bee solde at the Greyhound in Paules-Church-yard, by *W. W.*

The cover of John Smith's first book about Virginia, A True Relation.
This cover appears on an edition published in the mid-nineteenth century.

stole from the Englishmen. They tried to take everything they could seize, Smith complained. Those caught stealing were locked in the stockade and forced to attend the colony's morning and evening church services.

Smith met more hostility when he and eighteen men went upriver to the Chickahominy village to trade for food. "[W]ith as much scorn and insolency as they could express," he reported, the people there would not trade. The captain ordered his men to attack the village. Quickly, Smith recalled, the Chickahominy decided "to give up corn, fish, fowl, and what they had to make their peace."

Back in Jamestown, Newport and Ratcliffe both accused Smith of treating the Native Americans too harshly, a violation of the London Company's orders not to offend "the Naturals." However, Smith believed it was more important to keep two hundred colonists from starving than to follow rules made in London, so the president shrugged off this criticism. He knew that his severest critics, both Newport and Ratcliffe, were going back to England at the beginning of the year.

When Newport did leave, he took several hogsheads, or barrels, of corn from Jamestown's stores to feed his sailors. That left President Smith with the difficult task of finding more food.

8. Fighting for Food

THE JAMESTOWN COLONY DID NOT HAVE ENOUGH FOOD to last through winter. The Nansemonds, who lived a few miles downriver, had promised to send the colony 400 baskets of corn. This food would go a long way in helping the English survive until spring. When the shipment did not arrive by mid-December, Captain Smith led a band of armed men to their village. The frightened Nansemonds tried to keep them from coming ashore. Smith ordered his men to shoot at the Nansemonds. The musket fire did not kill anyone, but the flames, smoke, and noise sent the townspeople fleeing for cover. Smith and his men waded ashore, set fire to one wigwam, and threatened to burn the entire town.

The Nansemonds pleaded with the Englishmen to spare their homes and agreed to turn over half of their winter supply of food. They also promised, at Smith's insistence, to plant corn for the colony in the spring.

Powhatan knew the colonists faced starvation, so he sent a messenger to Jamestown to offer a deal. He would fill their barge with corn, but in return he wanted a grindstone, chickens, copper, glass beads, muskets, and swords. The werowance also wanted the English to build him a European-style house. Apparently Namontack had told him about the fine houses he had seen in London. Smith agreed and sent five of his best builders to Werowocomoco.

A few days later the president took forty-six men and the barge along with nearly a hundred pounds of copper and glass beads to trade. Snow and cold weather forced them to stop at Kecoughtan where they spent Christmas and the final days of 1608. According to Smith's notes, they were treated well. "[W]e were never more merry, nor fed on more plenty of good oysters, fish, flesh, wildfowl, and good bread, nor never had better fires in England than in the dry, warm, smoky houses of Kecoughtan."

The Englishmen arrived at Werowocomoco on January 12, 1609. Smith settled into a wigwam, and Powhatan immediately sent him platters of turkey, venison, and bread. The following day the two leaders began negotiations. Here, according to Smith, is how the discussion went:

"When are you leaving?" Powhatan asked. He didn't mind a friendly visit, but it was winter. Food was scarce for everyone.

"I'm here by your invitation," Smith reminded the werowance. "And I've agreed to your terms for trading."

"I don't want beads and copper," Powhatan said. "I want only muskets and hatchets."

Smith replied that he was disappointed that Powhatan had changed the terms of their agreement. But it wouldn't hurt their friendship, he emphasized; only bad treatment could damage that.

The werowance replied that he had heard about Smith's threats to the Nansemonds. "You frighten my people so much," he said, "that they dare not visit you." Powhatan did not trust the Englishmen. "[M]any do inform me

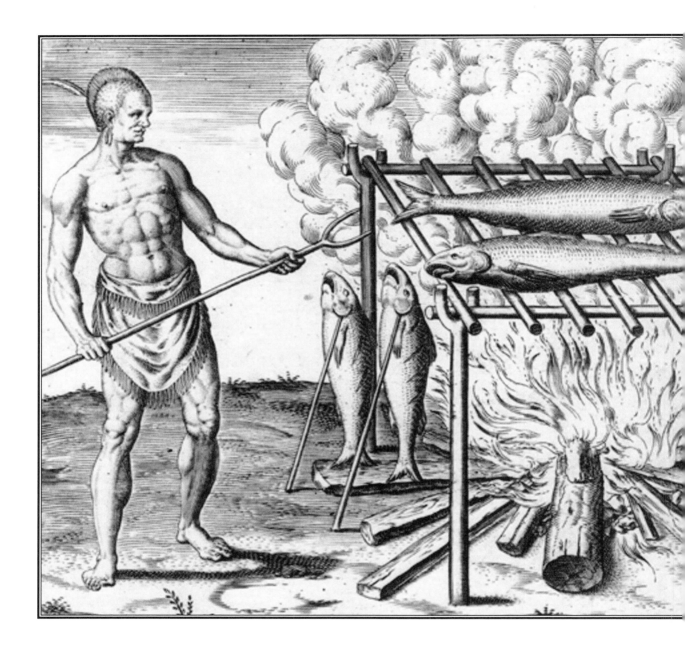

your coming hither is not for trade but to invade my people and possess my country."

The Algonquin chief explained that he had lived through terrible wars with other tribes. Now he only wanted peace for himself, his family, and his people.

Native Americans cooking fish.
Theodor de Bry made this engraving
based on a John White drawing.

They could be friends, but in the future Smith and his men could not come into his village armed.

Bearing arms, Smith replied, is not a sign of hostility. Yet he agreed to return the following day unarmed.

Powhatan then excused himself and went outside. Unknown to Smith, the werowance left Werowocomoco. The two men never saw one another again.

While the captain waited, warriors outside surrounded the wigwam. Smith's guards saw them and yelled a warning to the captain. Smith drew his

pistol and sword. Slashing right and left with his sword, he fled the wigwam.

The angry captain, his men standing behind him with their muskets raised, demanded food. The townspeople were afraid, so they grimly carried baskets of corn to the barge. They did not finish loading the barge until dusk. Despite

A drawing by John White of a Native American man and woman eating from a basket

the danger Smith and his men stayed another night at Werowocomoco.

That evening Smith had an unexpected visitor. Pocahontas snuck into his wigwam to warn him that her father planned to attack later that night. The captain thanked his young friend and offered her a gift. "[B]ut with the tears running down her cheeks," Smith related, "she ran away by herself as she came." The girl knew her father would kill even his favorite daughter if he discovered her betraying her people. Powhatan did not attack that night. Perhaps he saw that the Englishmen were well prepared to defend themselves.

The Englishmen next traveled to Opechancanough's village twenty-five miles up the Pamunkey River. After two days of feasting, they met to bargain. But Smith saw the warriors were armed with bows and clubs. They had learned, the captain realized, that Powhatan had broken off negotiations. Smith angrily told Opechancanough that he was sure the chief's people had plenty to eat. Then he reminded the chief that he had promised to send corn to Jamestown. Opechancanough reluctantly agreed to trade.

The next morning Smith and fifteen men went to Opechancanough's wigwam. Soon afterward one of the Englishmen ran in to report that dozens of warriors were gathering outside. The captain yelled to his men to stay calm, and then accused Opechancanough of treachery.

"I see, Opechancanough, your plot to murder me, but I fear it not." Smith proposed that just the two of them go to a nearby island and fight it out.

Opechancanough, perhaps fearing a trap, didn't like this idea. Instead he tried a trick of his own. He said he had a present for Smith, but he had to go outside to get it.

Smith reported that he suddenly "snatched the king by his long lock in the midst of his men, with his pistol ready bent against his breast. Thus he led the trembling king [near dead with fear] amongst all his people." Smith's rough

John Smith grabs Opechancanough. This drawing appeared in John Smith's
The General History of Virginia.

treatment of their werowance surprised the Pamunkey warriors. As a sign of submission, Opechancanough gave his bow to Smith, and then his warriors dropped their bows.

"I see, you Pamaunkees, the great desire you have to kill me," the captain shouted. "Shoot he that dare! You promised to fraught [load] my ship ere I departed, and so you shall or I mean to load her with your dead carcasses." Smith then switched to a friendlier tone of voice. "Yet if as friends you come and trade, I once more promise not to trouble you. . . ."

The Pamunkey people brought baskets of corn and venison. Afterward Opechancanough pretended that all was forgiven and prepared another feast for Smith.

The captain returned to Jamestown at the end of January with several hundred pounds of deer suet, or fat, and 479 bushels of corn. That was enough food to last the winter. But the colony's problems were far from over.

9. Smith's Last Summer

SOON AFTER SMITH LEFT WEROWOCOMOCO, Powhatan returned and plotted to steal weapons from Jamestown. He had help from three of the men building his European-style house. Adam, Franz, and Samuel had decided to betray their fellow colonists. It's not known why. They might have been swayed by the abundance of food. No doubt, as Powhatan's guests, the three men feasted on venison, turkey, and bread. Or, they might have been impressed by Powhatan's many warriors. Or, perhaps the werowance repeated an offer he had made to Smith earlier to share "the corn, women, and country" with them.

According to Smith's later estimate, Samuel had already stolen 300 hatchets, fifty swords, eight muskets and eight pikes. Powhatan wanted as many weapons as he could get. While Smith was at Opechancanough's village, Powhatan sent Adam and Franz to Jamestown with a phony story. They told Peter Winne, the man in charge of the arsenal, that Smith had taken their guns and they needed replacements. The story sounded reasonable, so Winne agreed. The two men also suggested to several unhappy colonists that they steal muskets, swords, pikes, shot, and gunpowder, and join them at Werowocomoco, "free from the miseries that would happen to the colony."

Franz and Adam waited. After a week went by with no word from the unhappy colonists, Franz slipped into Jamestown to find out why.

When President Smith returned to the fort, he learned that Franz had returned and sent several men to find him. Franz told the president that Powhatan had forced him and the other house-builders to stay in the village. There "was no small appearance of truth" in that explanation, Smith noted skeptically, and he ordered Franz locked in irons. Nothing more appears in Smith's notes about the other colonists who had agreed to help the builders.

The president, it seems, spent little time worrying about the conspirators; the colony needed to prepare for hundreds of newcomers expected that summer. Smith had long complained of "idleness and sloth" among the colonists. Now he was in a position to do something about it. He enacted strict rules. One stated, "He that will not work will not eat." The president posted an account of each worker's job performance on a public bulletin board. This public evaluation was intended to "encourage the good and with shame to spur on the rest." Despite lots of complaining, work began to get done.

Under Smith's orders the colonists dug a well inside the fort, put a new roof on the church, and built a guardhouse. The colony's hogs and chickens had multiplied. The colonists moved sixty pigs across the river to a spot they called, appropriately enough, Hog Island. The settlement was beginning to spread beyond James Island.

The winter of 1609 was unusually cold. Even the Native Americans suffered, in part because they had been forced to give much of their food to the English. The colonists discovered that black rats had eaten most of the stored corn. This was a problem the Native Americans did not have. Black rats and their cousins, brown rats, were unknown in the New World until they crossed the ocean from Europe on the same ships as colonists.

To survive, the Englishmen began adopting Native American ways. They made nets and weirs to catch fish; they hunted in the woods for turkey, deer, and other game; they dug up tuckahoe root to grind into flour to make Native-American-style bread.

The president still needed houses for the new colonists. A practical man, Smith was less interested in revenge than in the colony's survival. He sent William Henry Volda to Powhatan's village to offer the remaining house-builders a pardon if they would return to Jamestown to work.

But Volda proved untrustworthy, too. He was part of a conspiracy to overthrow Smith that was discovered when a pair of conspirators, Thomas Dowse and Thomas Mallard, changed their minds and confessed. Smith took firm action by sending two men to execute Volda and the builders.

When Powhatan learned that the would-be executioners were in his village, he demanded to know why. After hearing the explanation, the werowance promptly sent the president a message, denying all knowledge of the plot and saying it was okay with him to kill the house-builders. The arrival of a ship on July 2 disrupted the execution.

Samuel Argall, the ship's captain, had crossed the Atlantic by a new route north of the Caribbean islands. This route cut travel time from twelve or so weeks to only about seven weeks. More importantly Argall reported that King James had signed a second charter for the colony. The new charter added new investors, which gave the struggling company much-needed money. The new charter also reorganized the colony's government so that it would be led by several prominent Englishmen, including a lord-governor, Thomas West, 3rd Baron De La Warr, better known as Lord Delaware. Argall also said that the London Company had sent more supplies and colonists to Jamestown. A fleet of eight ships carrying over 500 men, women, and children, the third supply, had left England June 9. Six of those ships arrived on August 11, 1609. It had been a tough crossing. On one ship thirty-four people had died of sunstroke. A hurricane had blown two ships off course, including the fleet's flagship, the *Sea Venture*. On board were some 150 people, including Captain Christopher Newport and Jamestown's new deputy governor, Sir Thomas Gates.

Smith's foes, Archer and Ratcliffe, were on one of the six ships that had arrived. They immediately caused trouble by telling Smith he was no longer president. Smith wisely demanded to see a letter to that effect from the London Company. Because there was no letter and since many colonists supported Smith, he refused to yield the presidency until the new governor arrived.

The third supply increased the colony's population to over 400 people. Jamestown had become too crowded. To increase the chances of survival, the president decided to split the colony, just as the Native Americans split their towns when food was scarce in winter or during a drought.

Smith sent some sixty men under the command of John Martin to Point Comfort at the mouth of the Nansemond River where they could live by catching sturgeon and other fish. The newcomers immediately made enemies of the Nansemonds by attacking their town and killing many of the inhabitants. The Native Americans, intent on revenge, forced the Englishmen to abandon their Point Comfort outpost and return to crowded Jamestown.

Meanwhile Smith sent another 120 colonists, led by Francis West, seventy-

The title page of John Smith's The General History of Virginia, *a book about his explorations in the New World. Smith was one of Britain's leading proponents of colonization in America.*

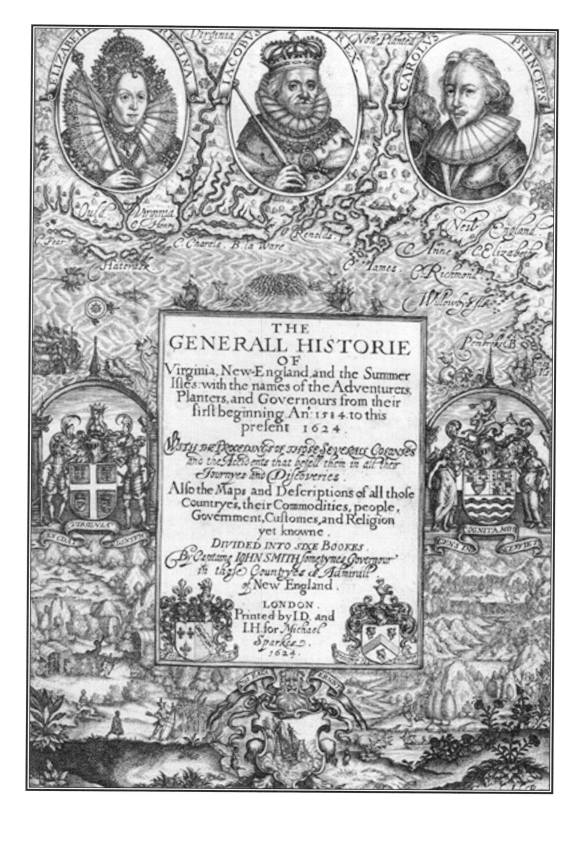

ELIZABETH REGINA · VIRGINIA · IACOBVS REX · Now Planted · CAROLVS PRINCEPS

THE
GENERALL HISTORIE
OF
Virginia, New-England, and the Summer
Isles: with the names of the Adventurers,
Planters, and Governours from their
first beginning. An: 1584. to this
present 1624.

With the Proceedings of those Severall Colonies
and the Accidents that befell them in all their
Journeys and Discoveries.

Also the Maps and Descriptions of all those
Countryes, their Commodities, people,
Government, Customes, and Religion
yet knowne.

DIVIDED INTO SIXE BOOKES.

By Captaine IOHN SMITH sometymes Governour
in those Countryes & Admirall
of New England.

LONDON.
Printed by I.D. and
I.H. for Michael
Sparkes.
1624.

five miles up the James River to live at the falls. Soon afterward Smith visited the settlement and complained that it was too near the river, which flooded in winter. The president negotiated a deal with Pawatah to buy the hilltop village of Powhatan, but the colonists refused to move from their camp near the river. Tired of arguing, Smith gave up and left.

On the way downriver, the president stretched out in the barge to rest. Somehow, no one knows how, a match fell onto his lap and ignited a bag of gunpowder attached to Smith's belt. There was an explosion and a flash of flame. Smith jumped overboard to put out the fire. The other men pulled him from the river. The flesh on Smith's stomach and thighs had been burned off. "So grievous were his wounds and so cruel his torments," he recalled, that he expected to die.

The council, which now included Archer, Ratcliffe, and Martin, appointed George Percy to replace the injured president. Smith did not die from the gunpowder burn, but he decided to return to England in September.

Even then his enemies were not finished. They wrote a letter to the directors of the London Company, claiming Smith abused both Native Americans and colonists. They also charged that he intended to marry Pocahontas and set himself up as king.

The man responsible for the colony's survival and one of the few founders still alive never returned to Jamestown. Captain Smith led his last expedition in 1614. He explored the coast of present-day Maine and Massachusetts, which he named New England. Smith spent the rest of his life encouraging the colonization of America, calling it a "glorious possibility." John Smith died in 1631, but his writing survives to this day as the most important account of the founding of Jamestown.

Epilogue

AFTER SMITH'S DEPARTURE Jamestown continued to struggle and twice narrowly escaped destruction.

In late September of 1609, John Ratcliffe, accompanied by some fifty men, went to trade with Powhatan. The werowance had feared Smith. Now that he was gone, Powhatan tried to destroy the colony. Warriors ambushed the Englishmen, captured Ratcliffe, and tortured him to death.

That winter Powhatan kept Jamestown under siege. The four hundred men, women, and children crowded into the triangular fort quickly ran out of food. The winter of 1609 to 1610 was known as "the Starving Time." Desperately hungry, people ate dogs, cats, rats, snakes, toadstools, and horsehides. Colonists caught one man eating his dead wife and executed him. Other starving settlers ate a Native American's corpse, but were not punished. The following spring a ship docked at Jamestown where only sixty people were still alive. The survivors boarded the ship and abandoned the colony.

Near the Chesapeake, the vessel met two ships carrying the crew and colonists from the *Sea Venture*. They had been shipwrecked on a reef off Bermuda and had spent the winter there. The stranded settlers had used the wreckage of the *Sea Venture* to build two smaller ships, *Patience* and *Deliver-*

ance, and sail to Jamestown. Lord Delaware arrived on another ship that summer. He imposed strict discipline on the colony and led attacks against the Native Americans, burning towns and killing hundreds of people.

In 1611 Sir Thomas Dale started a new settlement called Henrico, some forty miles upriver from Jamestown. Hundreds of colonists moved there, leaving only a few dozen people at Jamestown.

The following year Englishmen kidnapped Pocahontas. While a prisoner she converted to Christianity, took the name Rebecca, and married the colonist John Rolfe. Pocahontas; Rolfe; and their son, Thomas, visited England in 1616 for seven months. Just before sailing back to Virginia, Pocahontas became sick and died.

When John Smith returned to England in 1609, he learned that the London Company had great "confidence and trust" in his leadership. The council members had even appointed the captain second in command of the Jamestown colony, but he did not accept the job.

Despite the efforts of John Smith and of many others, few English people wanted to migrate to the New World in the early 1600s. The London Company gave free passage to colonists who agreed to work seven years as indentured servants. For many years over half of the migrants to Virginia were indentured men and women. The struggling colony also attracted migrants by a headright system. This was an incentive of fifty acres of land for each newcomer, or anyone who paid a newcomer's passage.

One of the most important developments for the English colony was the cultivation of tobacco. The Native Americans grew tobacco, but its smoke was harsh. John Rolfe, who arrived in Jamestown in 1610 with the colonists from the shipwrecked *Sea Venture,* imported seeds from the West Indian island of

A 1616 engraving of Pocahontas by Simon van de Pass is the only portrait of Pocahontas made within her lifetime.

A drawing by Howard Pyle in Harper's *magazine in* 1901 *imagines the first Africans in British North America sold at Jamestown by a Dutch slave trader.*

Trinidad that produced plants with milder smoke. The Chesapeake climate and soil proved excellent for growing tobacco. It quickly became the region's most important crop, and plantations sprang up all around the Chesapeake Bay.

The year 1619 was significant for Jamestown for three reasons: First, the London Company sent one hundred women to the colony. Men purchased them as wives for 120 pounds of tobacco each. Families were essential for the colony's stability and growth.

The second significant event occurred on July 30 when elected delegates, called burgesses, met with the royal governor and the council in the Jamestown Church to enact laws for the colony. This meeting marked the beginning of the House of Burgesses. It was the first representative assembly in the New World and a modest beginning of democratic government in America.

The third significant event of 1619 was the arrival in August of a Dutch ship with some "twenty and odd Negroes." They were the first Africans in British North America. Slave traders found a steady market in Virginia because the tobacco plantations needed large numbers of laborers. By the end of the century, there were thousands of Africans and their descendents in the colonies, and slavery was firmly established.

Fighting between the colonists and the Native Americans continued for decades, even after Powhatan died of old age in 1618. His half brother, Opechancanough, planned one of the most successful attacks against the colonists in Native American history. Early on March 22, 1622, hundreds of warriors surprised the outlying plantations, killing 350 men, women, and children. An Algonquin boy named Chaco warned the people at Jamestown, and they were able to fight off the attackers. The English retaliated, killing hundreds of Native Americans, and driving survivors far to the west, away from the expanding settlements.

In 1624 King James I took control of the colony and its 1,300 residents

from the bankrupt London Company. With a stable sponsor, the Native American threat suppressed, and tobacco as a cash crop, Jamestown's survival appeared assured. But it had come at a high price. In just eighteen years,

Theodor de Bry's engraving of the Jamestown massacre of 1622

between 1607 and 1625, some 8,500 people migrated to Jamestown, but 7,200 of them died from war, starvation, or disease.

The Jamestown settlers never achieved their original goals of finding gold, rescuing survivors of the Lost Colony, discovering the northwest passage, and converting the Native Americans to Christianity. But those men and boys who founded Jamestown prepared the way for millions of Europeans——the biggest migration in world history——who would immigrate to America, seeking more personal freedom and more economic opportunities than they had at home. Today, four hundred years later, ambitious people from all over the world still come to America seeking personal freedom and better futures.

Time Line

1492	Christopher Columbus makes his first voyage to the New World.
1497	John Cabot explores the land now called Canada.
1587	John White settles over one hundred colonists on Roanoke Island and sails back to England for supplies.
1590	Returning to Roanoke, John White finds no people and no houses. Roanoke becomes known as the Lost Colony.
1606	The Virginia Company of London receives its first charter.
1606	In December, Christopher Newport and his fleet sail for Virginia.
1607	In April, the fleet's three ships arrive at the mouth of the Chesapeake Bay.
1607	In May, the Englishmen establish their colony on James Island.
1607	In May, Newport and Smith explore the James River.
1607	In December, Smith is captured and meets Powhatan and Pocahontas.
1608	In January, Smith returns to Jamestown where he is condemned to be executed but saved by Captain Newport's arrival.
1608	In January, the first supply arrives.
1608	In September, Smith becomes Jamestown's president.
1608	In September, the second supply arrives.
1608	In October, the English hold a coronation for Powhatan.

1609	In May, the London Company receives a second charter.
1609	In August, the third supply arrives.
1609	In September, Smith is injured and leaves Virginia.
1609	"The Starving Time" begins during the winter.
1610	The missing ships of the third supply arrive. Delaware arrives on a separate ship.
1611	In September, Henrico is established.
1614	Pocahontas marries John Rolfe.
1618	Powhatan dies.
1619	In July, the London Company sends one hundred women to Jamestown.
1619	In August, twenty Africans are brought to Virginia.
1619	In August, the Virginia House of Burgesses, the first representative assembly in America, meets in Jamestown.
1622	Native Americans attack Jamestown, killing 350 people.
1624	In May, the London Company's charter is revoked, and Jamestown becomes a royal colony.

Algonquin Words That Became Common English Words

According to historian Edward Wright Haile, the Algonquin language spoken by Powhatan's people contributed more words to American English than any other Native American language. Here are a few of the words once spoken by Powhatan and his people that we speak today.

hickory

moccasin

persimmon

raccoon

tomahawk

hominy

opossum

pokeberry

terrapin

hickory

terrapin

George Percy's Description of Powhatan's People

Observations gathered out of a Discourse of the Plantation of the Southerne Colonie in Virginia by the English, 1606. Written by that Honorable Gentleman, Master George Percy.

When we came first a Land they made a dolefull noise, laying their faces to the ground, scratching the earth with their nailes. We did thinke that they had beene at their Idolatry. When they had ended their Ceremonies, they went into their houses and brought out mats and laid upon the ground, the chiefest of them sate all in a rank: the meanest sort brought us such dainties as they had, & of their bread which they made of their Maiz or Gennea wheat, they would not suffer us to eat unlesse we sate down, which we did on a Mat right against them. After we were well satisfied they gave us of their Tabacco, which they tooke in a pipe made artificially of earth as ours are, but far bigger, with the bowle fashioned together with a piece of fine copper. After they had feasted us, they shewed us, in welcome, their manner of dancing, which was in this fashion: one of the Savages standing in the midst singing, beating one hand against another, all the rest dancing about him, shouting, howling, and stamping against the ground, with many Anticke tricks and faces, making noise like so many Wolves and Devils. One thing of them I observed; when they were in their dance they kept stroke with their feet just one with another, but with their hands, heads, faces, and bodies, every one of them had a severall gesture: so they continued for the space of halfe an houre. When they had ended their dance, the Captaine gave them Beades and other trifling Jewells. They hang through their eares Fowles legs:

they shave the right side of their heads with a shell, the left side they weare of an ell long tied up with an artificiall knot, with a many of Foules feathers sticking in it. They goe altogether naked, but their privities are covered with Beasts skinnes beset commonly with little bones, or beasts teeth: some paint their bodies blacke, some red, with artificiall knots of sundry lively colours, very beautifull and pleasing to the eye, in a braver fashion than they in the West Indies.

Source Notes

The following notes are mainly citations of the sources of quoted materials in this book. A few of the notes are for the sources of some statistics. All of the books listed below are mentioned in Sources at the back of this book.

1. *The First Day in the Country Called Virginia*

p. 5   "sixth and twentieth day . . .": *Jamestown Narratives*, p. 90.

p. 11   "Paradise. . . . Fair meadows . . .": *Jamestown Narratives*, p. 90.

            "Savages. . . . After they had spent . . .": *Jamestown Narratives*, p. 90.

2. *A Glorious Possibility*

p. 12   The number of people on the three ships comes from *Three Worlds*, p. 113.

p. 16   "to usurp the government . . .": *Jamestown Narratives*, p. 225.

            "paire of gallowes . . .": *Three Worlds*, p. 116.

p. 17   "son of a poor tenant": *Three Worlds*, p. 93.

            "glorious possibility": *Three Worlds*, p. 93.

p. 19   "entertained by them very kindly": *Jamestown Narratives*, p. 91.

            "a very fit place . . .": *Three Worlds*, p. 125.

p. 20   "not to offend the Naturals": *Pocahontas*, p. 26.

3. *Looking for Gold*

p. 21   "a Fat Deare as a gift": *Jamestown Narratives*, p. 95.

p. 22   "They came more in villainy . . .": *Jamestown Narratives*, p. 95.

p. 22   "Thus from James Fort . . .": *Jamestown Narratives*, p. 103.

p. 23   "They live commonly by the waterside . . .": *Jamestown Narratives*, p. 123.
"an oration . . . entertained us. . . . against the ground . . .": *Jamestown Narratives*, p. 125.

pp. 23–25   "privities with beasts skins. . . . very beautiful . . .": *Jamestown Narratives*, p. 92.

p. 25   "came to an overfall. . . .": *Jamestown Narratives*, p. 107.
"terrify and kill": *Jamestown Narratives*, p. 111.

pp. 25–26   "stop'd his ears. . . . never use . . .": *Jamestown Narratives*, p. 111.

p. 26   "veins of glistering spangles": *Three Worlds*, p. 131.
"We saw the queen. . . . She is a fat . . .": *Jamestown Narratives*, p. 112.

p. 28   "some mischief at the Fort": *Three Worlds*, p. 135.
"to doe naturall necessity": *Pocahontas*, p. 62.
"country is excellent and very rich . . .": *Jamestown Narratives*, p. 130.

4. Such Misery

p. 29   "There was never Englishmen. . . . The fourteenth day . . .": *Jamestown Narratives*, pp. 99—100.

pp. 29–30   "Our food. . . . the destruction . . .": *Jamestown Narratives*, p. 100.

p. 30   "It pleased god . . .": *Jamestown Narratives*, p. 100.
"They would rather starve . . .": *Three Worlds*, p. 149.
"Though there be fish . . .": *Complete Works of Captain John Smith*, p. 188.
"of feasting himself": *Three Worlds*, p. 145.

5. Facing the Great Chief

p. 32   This account of Cassen's death came from Smith, who apparently heard it from his captors. *Jamestown Narratives*, p. 157.

p. 35   "Each morning three women presented me . . .": *Jamestown Narratives*, p. 154.
"[T]heir emperour proudly lying . . .": *Jamestown Narratives*, p. 160.

p. 37   "his head in her arms . . .": *Jamestown Narratives*, p. 239. This is Smith's description of the event. Some historians doubt his account because he did not write about the incident until fifteen years later. Other historians believe this might have been an adoption ritual, making Smith an honorary werowance.

"most dolefullest noise. . . . like a devil . . .": *Jamestown Narratives*, p. 240.

pp. 37–39   "sent me home . . .": *Jamestown Narratives*, p. 162.

p. 39   "Greate. . . . But in the midst . . .": *Jamestown Narratives*, p. 164.

6. Cursed Gold

p. 41   "Many of our old men . . .": *Jamestown Narratives*, p. 165.

pp. 41–42   "The Emperor Powhatan each week . . .": *Jamestown Narratives*, p. 165.

p. 42   "[V]ictuals, you must know . . .": *Jamestown Narratives*, p. 168.

"child of ten . . .": *Jamestown Narratives*, p. 181.

"Before his house . . .": *Jamestown Narratives*, p. 166.

"This proud savage . . .": *Jamestown Narratives*, p. 166.

p. 44   "the corn, women, and country": *Jamestown Narratives*, p. 167.

"a shrew's subtle capacity . . .": *Jamestown Narratives*, p. 245.

pp. 44–45   "was no talke, no hope, no worke . . .": *Jamestown Narratives*, p. 247.

pp. 45–47   "extreme thick full of wolves . . . a bad instrument to catch fish with": *Jamestown Narratives*, p. 262.

pp. 47–48   "torment was so . . .": *Jamestown Narratives*, p. 263.

7. Powhatan's Strange Coronation

p. 52   "For we had his favor . . .": *Jamestown Narratives*, p. 279.

p. 55   "[W]ith as much scorn. . . . to give up corn . . .": *Jamestown Narratives*, p. 285.

8. Fighting for Food

p. 57   "[W]e were never more merry . . .": *Jamestown Narratives*, p. 297.

p. 57 Powhatan's and Smith's discussion: *Jamestown Narratives*, pp. 297—300.

pp. 57–58 "[M]any do inform me . . .": *Jamestown Narratives*, p. 298.

p. 62 "[B]ut with the tears running down . . .": *Jamestown Narratives*, p. 303.

"I see, Opechancanough . . .": *Jamestown Narratives*, p. 306.

"snatched the king . . .": *Jamestown Narratives*, p. 307.

p. 64 "I see. . . . Yet if as friends . . .": *Jamestown Narratives*, p. 307.

9. *Smith's Last Summer*

p. 65 "the corn, women, and country": *Jamestown Narratives*, p. 167.

"free from the miseries . . .": *Jamestown Narratives*, p. 312.

p. 66 "was no small appearance": *Three Worlds*, p. 260.

"idleness and sloth": *Jamestown Narratives*, p. 314.

"He that will not work . . . encourage the good . . .": *Jamestown Narratives*, p. 314.

p. 70 "So grievous were his wounds . . .": *Jamestown Narratives*, p. 333.

Epilogue

p. 72 "confidence and trust": *Three Worlds*, p. 286.

p. 75 "twenty and odd Negroes": *American History*, p. 33.

Sources

This book relies a great deal on primary sources, or the writings of people who were at Jamestown, especially the notes and recollections of Captain John Smith.

The first three chapters are drawn from the first report Smith sent back to England in the summer of 1608. The commonly used short title of that report is *A True Relation*. The document's complete title is *A True Relation of Such Occurrences and Accidents of Noate as Hath Hapned in Virginia Since the First Planting of that Collony, which is now resident in the South part thereof, till the last returne from thence. Written by Captaine Smith one of the said Collony, to a worshipfull friend of his in England*, and is reprinted in Edward Wright Haile's *Jamestown Narratives*.

Other colonists left brief records. In my early chapters, I use many quotes from George Percy's *Observations gathered out of "a discourse of the plantation of the southern colony in Virginia by the English 1606."* Also helpful, especially for Chapter 3, was *A Relation of the Discovery of our river from James Fort into the Main, made by Captain Christopher Newport, and sincerely written and observed by a gentleman of the colony.* The author is generally believed to have been Gabriel Archer. Both of these records are reprinted in Haile's *Jamestown Narratives*.

For information on the second year at Jamestown, I relied on book three in John Smith's six volume *The General History of Virginia, New England and the Summer Isles,* published in 1624. Additional primary documents for early Jamestown are scarce. The biggest gap is the lack of information from the Native Americans. Everything known about Powhatan's people comes from Europeans who knew little about their language or culture.

An indispensable secondary source is by Philip L. Barbour. The historian and writer spent years studying the life of John Smith, including extensive research in Europe. Barbour collected all of Smith's writings in *The Complete Works of Captain John Smith* [1580—1631] [Chapel Hill: University of North Carolina Press, 1986]. He also published two informative biographies, *The Three Worlds of Captain John Smith* [Boston: Houghton Mifflin, 1964] and *Pocahontas and Her World* [Boston: Houghton Mifflin, 1970].

A third important source is Edward Wright Haile's *Jamestown Narratives—Eyewitness Accounts of the Virginia Colony, The First Decade: 1607—1617* [Champlain, Va. per cms: RoundHouse, 1998]. Haile compiled this collection in anticipation of the four hundredth anniversary of the founding of Jamestown. Haile has done a service for readers by updating the writings of Smith, Percy, and others into modern English. Most of the quotes in this book are from Haile's modern versions of the primary sources.

Other secondary works include Carl Bridenbaugh's *Jamestown 1544—1699* [New York: Oxford University Press, 1980]; Frederic W. Gleach's *Powhatan's World and Colonial Virginia: A Conflict of Cultures* [Lincoln: University of Nebraska Press, 1997]; Frances Mossiker's *Pocahontas: The Life and the Legend* [Reprint, New York: Da Capo Press, 1996]; Helen C. Roundtree's *The Powhatan Indians of Virginia* [Reprint, Norman: University of Oklahoma Press, 1992]; Alden T. Vaughan *American Genesis: Captain John Smith and the Founding of Virginia* [Boston: Little Brown, 1975].

My sources for overviews and for checking facts include *Microsoft's Encarta 2005 Reference Library Premium CD* [Microsoft Corporation, 2004]; Alan Brinkley's text *American History*, eighth edition [New York: McGraw-Hill, 1991]; *The Reader's Companion to American History*, edited by John A. Garraty and Eric Foner [Boston: Houghton Mifflin, 1991]; and *The Almanac of American History*, edited by Arthur M. Schlesinger, Jr. [New York: Putnam, 1983].

Illustration Sources

Many of the illustrations are from original images by John White. White was among the colonists who in 1485 planted the first English colony on Roanoke Island. During thirteen months there, White made some 70 drawings and watercolors of the daily lives of the Native men, women and children who, like the Chesapeake Native Americans, were Algonquin. Their language and customs were similar. A printer named Thedor De Bry later published a popular book of etchings from White's drawings. The original White watercolors are in the British Library in London, England. Photographic reproductions are available from the British Library, the Library of Congress, and the Library of Virginia.

Additional Reading

Doherty, Kieran. *To Conquer is to Live: The Life of Captain John Smith of Jamestown.* Brookfield, Conn.: Twenty-First Century Books, 2001.

Fritz, Jean. *The Double Life of Pocahontas.* New York: Puffin Books, 1987.

Karwoski, Gail. *Miracle: The True Story of the Wreck of the* Sea Venture. Plain City, Ohio: Darby Creek Publishing, 2004.

Riehecky, Janet. *The Settling of Jamestown.* Milwaukee: World Almanac Library, 2002.

Sewall, Marcia. *James Towne: Struggle for Survival.* New York: Atheneum Books for Young Readers, 2001.

Internet Sites

The Association for the Preservation of Virginia Antiquities' *Jamestown Rediscovery* is a decade-long archaeological project digging up artifacts of the original colony: www.apva.org/jr.html

The official site for the Colonial Historical Park operated by the National Park Service has information about the history of Jamestown and about visiting the original site and the recreated village: www.nps.gov/jame

Virtual Jamestown is a treasure chest of firsthand accounts, maps, and other primary materials about the colony: www.virtualjamestown.org

Picture Credits

The prints and maps in this book are all used with permission from the following sources:

Index

Page numbers in *italic* type refer to illustrations

Powhatan [werowance, or chief] *[continued]*:
 Newport's first meeting with, 44
 Smith adopted as son by, 37
 Smith's meetings with, 31, 32, 35–37, 42–44,
  57–60
 weapons sought by, 37, 56, 57, 65–66
 wigwam of, 35
Pyle, Howard, 74

Raleigh, Sir Walter, 3, 4, 11
Ratcliffe, John, 5, 19, 31, 39, 48, 55, 68, 70, 71
rats, 66
Read, James, 31
Roanoke Island, 22, 90
 Lost Colony of, 4, 21, 49, 78
 map of, 2–3
Robinson, John, 32, 34, 39
Rolfe, John, 72–75
Rolfe, Thomas, 72

St. Augustine settlement, 1
Samuel [colonist], 65, 67
Savage, Thomas, 44
scalp lock, 23
Scrivener [councilman], 48
Sea Venture, 68, 71, 72
Secota, 27
silver, 1, 14
slave trade, 74, 75
Smith, John, 19, 32–48
 adopted as son by Powhatan, 37

Algonquin language studied by, 22
Chesapeake Bay explored and mapped by, 45–48,
 46–47
conspiracy aimed at overthrow of, 67
early career of, 17
family background of, 17
food supply and, 31, 41–42, 44, 52, 55, 56–64
The General History of Virginia by, 33, 34, 38, 63,
 69
in governing council, 20, 22, 30–31, 48
housebuilders' plot to steal weapons and, 65–66,
 67
injured by gunpowder explosion, 70
Jamestown colony split into two settlements by,
 68–70
Jamestown left by, 70
laziness ascribed to Jamestown settlers by, 30,
 66
Nantaquaus as Algonquin name of, 37
Opechancanough's murder plot against, 62–64,
 63
Pocahontas's rescue of, 37, 38
portrait of, 18
Powhatan's coronation and, 49, 52
Powhatan's meetings with, 31, 32, 35–37, 42–44,
 57–60
as president of Jamestown, 48, 49, 68, 70
quest for gold and, 26, 42, 44–45
rules of conduct imposed by, 66
taken captive by Opechancanough, 32–35, 34
trial and near-execution of, 39, 40